2022
World Cup
Devotional

2022
World Cup
Devotional

The Light Is
Coming

2022 World Cup Devotional | The Light is Coming
Copyright © 2022 Soccer Chaplains United

ISBN: 9798356271502

Editor: Jan van Vliet, PhD

Kickoff Author: Rev Bradly Michael Kenney
Halftime Author: Rev Jordan Medas
Final Whistle Author: Pastor Kurt Trempert

Illustrators: Stella Bertsch, Caley Kenney, and Kiera Thielke
Interior Design: Jubal McDaniel
Cover Design: Jim Barnard and Bradly Michael Kenney

This edition is self-published through KDP
First printing edition 2022

Dedication

To all who love the Beautiful Game

And to all who are loved by the One who
made the Beautiful Game

Table of Contents

Introduction

Welcome to the Soccer Chaplains United 2022 World Cup Devotional | *The Light Is Coming*. This book covers the seasons of Advent and Christmas. Celtic and Orthodox observances of Advent begin 40 days prior (November 15) to Christmas Day. All of this coincides wonderfully with the 22nd FIFA World Cup in Qatar — the first time the tournament has been played during this time of year.

Advent originally began as a mirror to Lent (40 days before Easter). The word comes from the Latin *'adventus'* meaning *'arrival.'* This intentional time helps us better reflect, celebrate, and anticipate the three arrivals of Jesus.

What do we mean by **three** arrivals of Jesus?

The first was his birth some 2000 years ago. Jesus' third arrival is his promised return at the end of this age. His *"second"* coming is when he personally enters into our heart and life as we repent of sin, surrender control, and seek to follow him. His second coming isn't just a one-time event, it's a daily, on-going exercise. Not everyone will experience his second coming. Jesus doesn't force his way into our lives. Scripture says, *"...I stand at the door and knock..."* (Revelation 3:20). Jesus waits for us to let him in.

This year, as we enjoy the World Cup, may we all experience the second *adventus* of Jesus — perhaps his most important arrival. We pray this devotional sparks a new interest, curiosity, and strength in your faith, family, and your football. Blessings on the journey! Blessings on the World Cup!

A Daily Prayer

God of all who wait,
God of all who hope,
Prepare within my heart
A way for entering in,
For letting Your Light penetrate my darkness.
Let me grow in faith,
Each and every minute —
Each and every day.
That I might take great joy,
That I may take great delight
In knowing that You love me,
In knowing that You offer me peace,
And in knowing that I ought to do the same.
I bring all of me —
Every bit that's broken and bruised,
Every bit that's excellent and wonderful —
And I worship, You.
You alone are worthy of all glory and honor.
I worship, You.
Amen

Silence and Waiting
Week One

Nov 13 — 19

(FIFA Roster Release and Advent Begins)

The Long Wait

How well do we wait for things? How about for a match to begin? Injury recovery? An agent callback? A new contract or scholarship award? A national team call-up? A passport? The list and lengths of waiting seem endless at times.

Week 1 | Kickoff

Romans 8:19;

Revelation 8:1

"The creation waits in eager expectation for the children of God to be revealed."

—

"When he opened the seventh seal, there was silence in heaven for about half an hour."

Can you believe that a people once waited over 400 years? They were waiting to hear from God. They were waiting for rescue, for a Champion. They were waiting for a win. All they received in return, though, was silence.

Silence and waiting seem to go hand in hand. Waiting's hard — whether it's three pulsating little dots on a text thread or waiting for a child's birth. Silence is often an indicator that something is about to happen. Think about the calm or silence before a storm. In Revelation 8, we see silence is a precursor to something amazing about to happen — Jesus' return.

Four hundred years of silence preceded Jesus' first coming. God didn't speak to His people — not through prophets, not through scripture. It was a unique time in the history of God and humanity. A long period of time. But could we endure 400 years of silence, 400 years of waiting?

Today, there are still 134 countries that have never qualified for the World Cup. Luxembourg carries the dubious distinction for the longest run of failed qualification.

Dating back to 1934, this small, Western European country has watched 20 attempts fall short (Finland ranks second with 19). For these nations, perhaps hope that the expanded, 2026 edition of the World Cup will finally see them in the tournament. If Luxembourg qualifies, it will be 92 years of waiting. That's a long time.

Waiting and silence seem (to me) to be tempered, made more tolerable, by one thing — the people who wait with us. I heard it once said that you could tell the nature of a true friend by their ability to be present and <u>silent</u> in times of waiting — the ability to companion someone without a need for words. Who waits with you and me in the silence? A parent, a partner, a friend? Have you ever felt God's presence in the midst of waiting? What was that experience like? What does silence make you believe (or disbelieve) about God? About faith?

This week, let the spiritual themes of silence and waiting serve as touchlines of a pitch. Perhaps some old issues of faith and belief arise. Maybe some old wounds and hard memories surface. Don't ignore them. Throw them back in; wrestle, juggle, and struggle with them, if need be. And do this in community — with a trusted friend, teammate, coach, parent, pastor, or chaplain.

This week, consider people in the Bible who have learned to wait, who have learned to live with silence. People like the nation of Israel. Like them, as you and I encounter our own silence and waiting spaces, may we not lose hope, may we keep watch, may we prepare, and may we keep faith.

~ Rev Brad

Waiting Is Good?

This 400 years for which God's people had to wait to hear from Him is called the *"intertestamental period"* — from the end of the Old Testament book of Malachi, to the birth of Jesus the Messiah in Bethlehem as recorded in the Gospels of Matthew and Luke. If God made His people wait to hear from Him, He had a purpose in doing so.

**Week 1 |
Halftime**

Read the book of
Malachi

—

*"Waiting is a period
of learning. The
longer we wait, the
more we hear about
him for whom we are
waiting."*

- Henri Nouwen

Much like children who always get what they want when they want it, if we don't spend time in anticipation, anxiously waiting for something desired, and reflecting on why we desire it, do we fully appreciate that which we desire?

We've waited a little over 4 years for this World Cup. Aren't you glad we didn't have to wait 400 years? Would we even remember the World Cup after 50 to 100 years? The truth is, whether we like it or not, waiting is good.

But why is waiting good?

- Waiting naturally gives us time to slow down and rest. Our hearts, bodies, minds, and souls need down time to refresh and recuperate.
- Waiting helps us take notice of the things around us that we normally do not have time to appreciate. When we're always on the go, the beauty of the things and people around us pass us by in a blur. Waiting

helps us notice the beauty in the everyday things God has put in our lives.

- Waiting helps us focus on that which we really want. If, after time to process and evaluate our wants, something is still on our heart, there is a good chance it's worthy of pursuit.

- Waiting creates space. We've all heard it time and time again in practice and during games: *create space.* Waiting gives us the opportunity to create space to take inventory of our past, evaluate our present, and prepare for the future.

Advent is a season of preparation as we celebrate the birth of the Savior of the world, Jesus Christ, as well as the expectation of his return. But if we don't take time to wait, be silent, and ponder that which, or in this case whom, we are celebrating, are we truly prepared to celebrate? Or are we merely going through the motions of tradition? Or even worse, are we celebrating the tradition instead of the reason for that tradition?

My encouragement today is that during this Advent season, take the moments given to you, whether from travel, natural down time, or in recovery/recuperation, to create space and take inventory of where you've been in life, where you are now, and what God has in store for you. Take that space to ponder what it means that God came to be with us, live among us, walk with us, dine with us . . . all because of His great love for us.

~ Rev Jordan

15

Waiting Sucks! But...

I love my microwave, my cell phone, my convection oven, and my car. I prefer to fly over driving; and if I could afford it, I would rather take a sub-orbital flight across the ocean. All of these illustrate my abhorrence of waiting. If it is available now, then I want access to it.

As I have grown older and the gray hair begins to appear, I have noted that my patience has developed as well. When I was a child, I could barely sit for ten minutes and wait for anything. As I have grown older, it seems that I have slowly entered a time-lapse continuum. It seems like yesterday my daughter was born, and I just walked her down the aisle a couple of weeks ago, presenting her to her new husband! What happened to time?

This first week of Advent is centered on the 400 years of waiting by the Hebrews. They were waiting for the Messiah to be revealed. They waited. For 400 years, they waited.

I don't know if you have ever been outside for an entire night waiting for the sun to rise, but let me tell you, it is always coldest just before the sun hits your face. You find yourself looking to the eastern sky with anticipation and longing — waiting for the Sun of Righteousness to rise with healing in His wings.

Anna and Simeon were two elderly people who went to the temple in Jerusalem daily in eager anticipation of the revelation of the Messiah to the people. They longed for Him. They were desperate for the healing of the nation and Jerusalem. I believe one of the reasons they were able to wait so patiently was because of their maturity — they had also entered that time-lapse continuum to which I referred. I believe this was possible through faith.

You probably also remember your childhood and how difficult it was to wait — whether it was waiting for Christmas morning, Three Kings' Day, or just waiting for your next meal. How do you practice the discipline of waiting now? As an adult, you must leave behind childish things, and one of those is impatience. Do not let your waiting turn into apathy, but learn what it means to intentionally wait — patience.

I would encourage you to be honest about what you are longing for with anticipation. How are you maturing through the process of waiting? What is God teaching you about Himself through this season of waiting and longing? Waiting sucks! But it is through waiting in faith that you learn about God's patience. And as children of our loving God we are admonished throughout the Christian scriptures to be like Him. To represent Him well. That gets better as we mature in the faith. That is why patience, faithfulness, and self-control are fruit of the Spirit — because waiting sucks and is not easy.

But take heart!

The final whistle will sound!   ~ Pastor Kurt

Preparation
Week Two

Nov 20 — 26

(Opening Game and Group Stage)

Prepare The Way

Today is the first match-day for the World Cup, but this day didn't just happen overnight — Qatar was announced as host on December 2, 2010. Preparations began nearly 12 full years ago! Seven new stadiums built (with air conditioning to combat the desert heat), a new airport, new transit system, and nearly 100 hotels — an entire city was built around Lusail Stadium, site of the final match!

In ancient times, preparations for the anticipated arrival of a king took place long before the journey began. A forerunner went in advance. He announced the king's coming and encouraged people to prepare. These *"encouragements"* weren't always friendly, either. Threats, violence, pain, punishment — those who lived along the travel routes had to prepare the way for the king, and if not ready in time, it could mean loss of life!

There were two main road fixes. The first was the raising up of low places (*every valley shall be raised up*). Over time, roadways developed holes, divots — *"potholes"* in our modern day. Essentially, the road was missing something necessary for smooth and safe passage. Ancient roadworks also included lowering high places (*every mountain and hill*

Week 2 | Kickoff

Matthew 3:3;
Isaiah 40:3b-4

"A voice of one calling in the desert, Prepare the way for the Lord, make straight paths for him."

—

"'...make straight in the wilderness a highway for our God. Every valley shall be raised up, every mountain and hill made low; the rough ground shall become level, the rugged places a plain.'"

made low). The king's road often had rocks and debris as obstacles that needed to be lowered, leveled, and removed.

Reflect on applying this to football, family, and faith. *What should I add to my football (a discipline, a skill)? Or what should I get rid of (bad habit, negativity, etc.)?*

Footballers should look at training and game preparation, as well as career preparation. Replacing a poor diet with healthy eating habits is one thing, but there is life after the game, too. Are you gambling, golfing, or gaming when you ought to be studying, learning, or earning coaching licenses? Imbalances and addictions are detrimental to athletic progression, mental health, sleep habits, and more.

Take the questions beyond football. *What is missing from my life that I need to add?* And *what in my life needs to be purged?* Be brave in asking and answering!

This week, whether preparing for match-day, pre-season, or the season itself — what does your readiness look like? Coach: your preparations may look different from athletes' but have similar timeframes and rhythms. Medical staff: your preparations must sync with strength/conditioning coaches. Scouts: what about your preparations? Some preparations are preventative. Others are restorative. Consider the differences!

Finally, **consider faith preparations**: Wrong ideas about God needing removal? Gaps in understanding how prayer works? Preconceptions about church/religion preventing from asking, exploring deeper questions? Now is the time to get ready, to prepare. Let mine be a voice calling: *Prepare the way!*

~ Rev Brad

Preparing The Heart

"Let's just go to the World Cup, the single biggest sporting event in the world, and rather than train and discuss tactics, let's just go out there on the pitch and see what happens!" What coach or manager has ever uttered such absurdity?

Week 2 | Halftime

Luke 3:4

"Isaiah had spoken of John [the Baptist] when he said, "He is a voice shouting in the wilderness, 'Prepare the way for the Lord's coming! Clear the road for him!'" (NLT)

—

"By failing to prepare, you are preparing to fail."

— Benjamin Franklin

It's ludicrous to imagine that after years of practice, study, conditioning, and qualifying that players and teams would leave their World Cup results to chance. Not even Ted Lasso would take that approach!

Advent is the season of the year when the church prepares to celebrate the birth or coming (*adventus*) of Jesus Christ (*Christmas*) and looks forward to his return one day in glory to judge the living and the dead. And while the preparations we usually think of this time of year include decorations, gatherings, and shopping, that's not the preparation that prophets such as Isaiah and John the Baptist are referring to. In anticipation of Christ's return, the preparations God calls us to include practices of self-examination and repentance.

The word repentance has, in some circles, fallen out of favor because of its negative connotation; however, the fact is that to be in communion with God, we must repent (turn away from) of our sin. Child Evangelism Fellowship defines sin as *"anything we think, say or do, that does not please God, or breaks God's laws."*

It may be surprising to you or it may come as no surprise at all that sin is real, and we all must address it in our own lives. That is how we prepare for the coming of Messiah, both his birth and his return: *"For everyone has sinned; we all fall short of God's glorious standard"* (Romans 3:23, NLT).

An oversimplified football analogy would be the player who, though he excels in many areas of the game, has a deficiency in his game that keeps him from being the player he could be (poor touch under pressure, trouble with situational awareness, lack of communication, etc.). The coach calls him out on it time after time, and the player says he will work on it; however, rather than acknowledging, addressing, and working on his deficiency, he denies its existence and pretends it doesn't affect his game. We all have deficiencies and shortcomings!

Because of Christ's coming, death on the cross for our sins, and victory over death in his resurrection, we can have *"life in abundance"* (John 10:10, NLT) and life eternal with God. *"For this is how God loved the world: He gave his one and only Son, so that everyone who believes in him will not perish but have eternal life"* (John 3:16, NLT).

This is why we celebrate Advent. When we prepare our hearts by acknowledging and addressing the sin in our lives, we truly come to understand the unspeakable joy that the coming of Christ Jesus the Messiah brings to those who know Christ as Lord and Savior of their lives.

~ Rev Jordan

Practice And Preparation

If we have heard it once, we have probably heard it a thousand times: *"Practice breeds confidence!"* Let us be clear, practicing the wrong thing does not help us meet our goals. Some practices breed failure! Sometimes you have to choose to change course, change a pattern, choose a new path, or just turn around.

I have been lost, but don't tell my wife or kids! Honestly, I really don't think I was ever lost; I just didn't know how to get to my destination. I have always known how to turn around and head back home. How frustrating it must be to not know your way home!

Many years ago, when I still played the Beautiful Game, one of my greatest downfalls was putting my head down and dribbling myself into a corner. I can still hear my coach yelling, *"Go Home! Go Home!"* Then the ball was taken away and I was playing defense again. If only I had listened to my coach, or better yet, if only I had paid more attention in practice to the tactic of *"Going Home"* instead of the skill of dribbling. I always assumed that I could just dribble my way out of a problem.

There are many times in our life that we need to hear someone, maybe a friend, a mentor, a coach, or a prophet,

---

Week 2 | Final Whistle

Luke 3:1-3

"In the fifteenth year...the word of God came to John son of Zechariah in the desert. He went into all of the country... preaching a baptism of repentance for the forgiveness of sins."

—

You can read about John the Baptist and his ministry in Luke 3:1-18

call for us to either, *"Go back!"* or, *"Go home!"* Have you found yourself in a corner with no way out except back the way you came? We all tend to put our head down and dribble into situations where there is no way out.

John the Baptist came to prepare the Hebrew people and also the Greeks (Gentiles) for the Messiah. His primary message was simple, *"Turn around! For the Kingdom of God is about to be revealed."* You see, the Hebrews had dribbled themselves into a corner of sin with no way out. John came to them and called out, *"Repent, turn around, and go home to what you know to be true,"* (my paraphrase). The Hebrews had given themselves over to the practice and ceremonies of religion and law-keeping in preparation for the coming of the Messiah only to realize that they were practicing the wrong things and being idolatrous.

True repentance addresses the whole person — the intellect, the heart or affections, and the will. The intellect **Recognizes** your sin; the heart feels **Remorse** over your shortcomings; and the will **Resolves** to abstain from ever repeating that thought, word, or deed again. True repentance sounds easy, doesn't it? But it is hard! And requires divine help to pull off successfully. But you have the Holy Spirit, who is eager and excited to help you in this task and align your life with God's desires once more.

What is a sin, an idol, a distraction that has you trapped in the corner with what seems like no way out? What would it look like for you to *"Go home!"*? Have you been practicing things that are not preparing you for life with Jesus?

~ Pastor Kurt

Hope
Week Three

Nov 27 – Dec 3

(Group Stage and Round of 16)

Hope Finishes Second?

This week's theme is hope. Undoubtedly, some nations have lost hope by now. Some have had two of three group stage matches played and will already understand their fate. Other teams, with two matches to go, will hold on to hope — even if game one didn't turn out as planned.

There's a reason hope comes in second. Hope, one of the big three theological Christian virtues, combines aspects of desire and expectation. Some believe it is a moral virtue. Some argue it is not. People often hope for things that are bad for the self and also bad for others. For example, someone might say: *"I hope that France does not win."*

Moral things — more specifically, moral *virtues* — are excellent attributes. If you're an English fan you might believe hoping France doesn't win is a good thing. But fans of *Les Bleus* believe a different story! Humankind is broken. Our hopes are broken — misaligned, misdirected, selfish.

Often, footballers hope for the starting lineup, but quickly add, *"Not that I hope anyone gets injured or anything…"* Hope often comes at the expense of others. We can also hope for things that are actually bad for us. Hope can seem very temporary and leave us unsatisfied. You've heard the saying: be careful what you wish (hope) for.

Despite all of these misappropriations of hope, when hope is placed into right things, it can be good for our souls. In Psalm 20, King David draws an important distinction between hope and trust. Trust is anchored in confidence. He contrasts those placing hope in chariots and horses with those trusting the living God. In ancient times, developing nations prized horses for warfare because of tactical advantages. Israel didn't develop horse and cavalry in its military until King Solomon (David's son). In fact, God actually commands (Joshua 11:6) the disabling of enemy warhorses by hamstringing — cutting the tendon above the ankle so a warhorse couldn't walk or run again. It seems odd, but God is helping His people place hope in Him.

Whether or not your team in the World Cup is fulfilling your hopes and dreams, we all have our *"horses,"* don't we? We fill out brackets, we guess scores and make predictions. We place hope in financial security, an educational pathway, a successful sports future, or a relationship.

But have we placed our hope and trust in God? Or is our hope in Him damaged by a painful past, a bad experience of church, a Christian who wronged us either deliberately or accidentally? Maybe we have a resilient hope because God has brought us through a battle with cancer or another adversity?

Hope in God is powerful because it is a transcendent hope — outside the bounds of physical, human limitation. God, in his wisdom, justice, and grace will provide for our needs and care for us, even if we are rooting against France.

~ Rev Brad

Hope Isn't A Fantasy

When the World Cup began two weeks ago, 832 of the world's best athletes (not to mention coaches, trainers, staff, and supporters back home) hoped to win the 2022 World Cup. The reality is only 26 players will lift the World Cup trophy on Dec. 18. Currently in the group stage, some players' hopes may still be alive while others' hopes may be a distant memory.

Perhaps we all too often confuse hopes with dreams and wishes. Dreams involve fantasizing about something greatly desired, and wishes involve something that probably will not or cannot be attained. Neither give assurance of coming to fruition. But hope, hope is defined as *"confident trust with the expectation of fulfillment."* It would be better to say that 832 players dream of winning or wish to win the 2022 World Cup. And there is absolutely nothing wrong with that dream or wish.

What an accomplishment to win such a prestigious award; however, for those who are in Christ, the Apostle Paul reminds us, *"Don't you realize that in a race everyone runs, but only one person gets the prize? So run to win! All athletes are disciplined in their training. They do it to win a prize that will fade away, but we do it for an eternal prize"* (I Corinthians 9:24-25, NLT). You dream of winning the World Cup, so you work hard to train and compete at an elite level. This is commendable, because you are to do everything as if for the Lord. But this Advent season I encourage you to look forward to the hope we have in Christ's coming, both in His birth and in His return.

There are about one hundred and twenty distinct prophecies of the first coming of the Messiah in the Old Testament. Here are a few: That he would be a descendent of Abraham (Genesis 12:3), from the tribe of Judah (Genesis 49:10), heir of David (Isaiah 9:6-7), born in Bethlehem (Micah 5:2), born of a virgin (Isaiah 7:14), declared the Son of God (Psalm 2:7), rejected by his own (Isaiah 53:3), betrayed by a friend (Psalm 41:9), and executed by crucifixion (Zechariah 12:10). Jesus fulfills each and every prophecy from the Old Testament. The chances of all these prophecies being fulfilled by one person is 1 in 84…**that is 1 in 84 x 10^{131}!**

For those in Christ, our hope is not in things of this world, but in God's Kingdom promises. *"So we fix our eyes not on what is seen, but on what is unseen, since what is seen is temporary, but what is unseen is eternal"* (2 Corinthians 4:18, NLT). Our hope is no mere wish or dream of life eternal, but the assurance that,

> *"Christ was born of the Virgin Mary, was crucified, died, and was buried. He descended to the dead. On the third day he rose again. He ascended into heaven and is seated at the right hand of the Father."*
> (From the Apostle's Creed)

That is our glorious hope!   **~ Rev Jordan**

Hope Deferred...Makes The Heart Sick

We all have had hopes for events or goals that have gone unmet. As we launch into this World Cup, every fan, team, player, coach, and nation has hope. For some, it is the hope that their team will just win one game, and for others, it is making it to the Round of 16. Every country (32) **hopes** that their team will bring the cup home.

To have hopes go unmet makes one sick. For many of us, in order to feel better, we just manage our hopes — knowing that we need to lower our expectations. We give up hoping, dreaming, or longing.

But, to have one's dream fulfilled — this is a tree of abundant life. Advent is intended to remind us of the hope that we have; but it is also a season of reflection and assessment. If we are honest, we realize that our hopes and dreams are placed in the wrong things or the wrong people. Advent by itself confronts this in each of us, and this year, the majority of the world is going to face severe disappointment.

But He came to give us abundance — not a World Cup! Though that would be nice, it is not even close to the abundance we can have in Jesus. In fact, Jesus said he didn't

Week 3 | Final Whistle

Proverbs 13:12

"Hope deferred makes the heart sick, but a longing fulfilled is a tree of life."

—

Take a moment to reflect on what your dreams are? Are you hoping for the right things? What steps are you taking to reach your goals? Is your hope in the right place or person?

come just to give us life, he said, *"I came that they may have life and have it abundantly"* (John 10:10, ESV). One could say it this way, *"I didn't come just to give you a World Cup, a perfect Christmas, or anything you dreamed of, I came to give you so much more!"*

Where have you and I placed our hope?

We need to take certain steps to take hold of the hope that we have. If we could already take hold of it completely, where would the hope be? But, because we have not seen it fulfilled yet, we hope for it. If our hope is not where it needs to be, it will only make us sick. If we are depending on the wrong person, event, or thing to satisfy and meet that hope, then it is an exercise in depression.

But the Christian scriptures teach hope in God as our personal good — namely, as the source of comfort and desire here on earth and perfect and lasting happiness in eternal life. That is why one of the great catechisms of the church begins with the opening question: *"What is the chief purpose of humanity?"* To which the answer is confident, hopeful, and resounding: *"To glorify God and enjoy him forever!"*

What if our hope was found in desiring to experience the abundant life promised by Jesus, and we were dependent upon Him for that? Would such hope be enough? How would that change our current life, our attitudes, our relationships? How does faith play into this?

More on that next week.

~ Pastor Kurt

Faith

Week Four

Dec 4 — 10

(Round of 16 and Third-place Match)

Faith Is In The Top Three

If your team has made it this far, the whisperings might have already started: *"You know, we just might win this thing..."* or *"The lads might be able to go all the way!"*

> **Week 4 | Kickoff**
>
> I Corinthians 13:13;
> Hebrews 11:1
>
> *"And now these three remain: faith, **hope** and love...the greatest of these is love."*
>
> —
>
> *"Now **faith** is being sure of what we hope for and certain of what we do not see."*

Sometimes when faith is about to become sight, we hold back hesitantly. We feel superstitious. We don't want to *"jinx"* a moment of sensing our team may be on the precipice of greatness. Certainly for the footballers striving and playing in the World Cup, a win will bring untold accolades, praise, and other earthly rewards. There's a part of us that wants to believe it, but also another part of us that doesn't want to believe it — we are afraid to believe it.

In the same way, we can sometimes express similar sentiments about God. If we do believe in God — well, that might just come at too high of a price, too hot to handle. I once asked a young footballer what he felt his biggest block or barrier was to actually believing in God. His answer? *"Well, if I do believe, and if He ends up being real, then He might make me give up something I really like and really enjoy."* He was worried God might have him give up football (among other things)! There are reasons we avoid believing in something. **Take a moment: write out or say aloud the blocks and barriers of faith for you.**

Hebrews 11:1 provides a compelling and distinct definition for understanding faith with two key elements:

surety and **certainty**. What do those words do, though, to our typical understanding of faith? Is faith merely blind acceptance, without any activity of the mind or will? Or do we see faith more diminutively, as in we just need the faith of a child? We prop up reasons and excuses for not growing or stretching faith *"muscles."* But words like **surety** and **certainty** aren't weak, wishful words. These are words and concepts of confidence that we may not normally associate with faith.

Today's scripture solidly locates faith in the top three Christian theological virtues for a reason. You see, faith is always realized, always seen. It is a reality in the here and now. Whereas hope is always **future-oriented**, faith is in the **present**. There's a day when faith ceases to be necessary — regardless of the outcome. It never stays a mystery. Faith in Jesus, for example, will one day become sight. In a moment — confirmation! Either Jesus is who he claims to be, or a lot of people will discover they've lived a good, moral life in vain.

So if faith is about **surety** and **certainty**, then where have we put our faith? What are we most sure about? Of what are we most certain? We all put our faith into something or someone, but do we have **surety** and **certainty**?

Today we might believe our national team will win the World Cup. Or we might be on the verge of another faithful moment becoming reality. Is our faith in those things characterized by **surety** and **certainty**? Do we realize we can have confidence and assurance when it comes to Jesus and to His Word?   **~ Rev Brad**

Sometimes, Faith Is All We Have

To get to the point of participating in a World Cup, you have probably put a lot of faith in a lot of people, processes, and resources. Faith in your youth coach to help you grow as a player. Faith in your trainers to keep you fit and performing at an elite level. Faith in the kit man to spell your name correctly. Faith in the formation, the tactics, and your coaches' choices for the starting eleven. Faith in the pilot who flew the plane to get you to Qatar. I bet if you took inventory of the number of people you put your faith in to get to this point, you would quickly lose count.

In the Bible, Mary, the mother of Jesus, put a lot of faith in her God. It took a lot of faith to come to terms with becoming pregnant through the power of the Holy Spirit. Joseph, likewise, put a lot of faith in the visitation from an angel who told him that Mary had conceived by the Holy Spirit, and he should not be afraid to take Mary as his wife. It took a lot of faith to continue being

---

Week 4 | Halftime

Matthew 17:20

"...if you have faith as small as a mustard seed, you can say to this mountain, 'Move'...and it will move. Nothing will be impossible for you."
(NLT)

—

"Faith is a living, bold trust in God's grace, so certain of God's favor that is would risk death a thousand times trusting in it. Such confidence and knowledge of God's grace makes you happy, joyful and bold in your relationship to God and all creatures."

— Martin Luther

engaged to a pregnant teenager in the ancient world.

Mary and Joseph are just two examples in the Bible of those putting their faith in God (see also Hebrews 11). But as Jesus said to his disciples, *"I tell you the truth, if you had faith even as small as a mustard seed, you could say to this mountain, 'Move from here to there,' and it would move. Nothing would be impossible"* (Matthew 17:20, NLT).

Sometimes faith is all we have. On the pitch, faith in our coaches and their ability to lead and make decisions that are the best for the national team. Faith in our teammates to give their all every time they're out on the pitch.

Throughout the Bible, God's people live life by faith. And that faith is not a blind faith, a dream, or wishful thinking. It is a faith grounded in the truths of God revealing himself to us in the Bible and in creation. Faith in a loving God who created you and sent his Son, Jesus Christ, to die for you. It's a faith that is expressed as, *"Christ was offered once for all time as a sacrifice to take away the sins of many people. He will come again, not to deal with our sins, but to bring salvation to all who are eagerly waiting for him"* (Hebrews 9:28, NLT).

So today, take heart! Find confidence in your faith. If you have put your faith in Christ Jesus as Lord, your faith has been credited to you as righteousness (Romans 4:3) and the Holy Spirit now dwells inside you to guide you and give you peace this day and forevermore.

~ Rev Jordan

Faith And Certainty

When we think of faith, we tend to understand it in the context of belief and truth comprehended by an exercise of our will. When we do this, it becomes next to impossible to live in a place of certainty. We find ourselves beating ourselves up as we try to will ourselves into a place of certainty — only to live in a place of condemnation.

Week 4 | Final Whistle

Hebrews 11:6

"And without faith it is impossible to please God, because everyone who comes to him must believe that he exists and the rewards those who earnestly seek him."

—

You can read about Mary and Zechariah's faith in Luke 1. You can read about many stories about faith in Hebrews 11.

However, what if faith was intended to be understood in the context of relationship, and we used words like trust, confidence, and faithfulness? Would it change anything? Would it change the way we read the Christmas story? I hope so, because then we would truly understand the deeper meaning of Christmas as demonstrating God's immeasurable love for his people through the provision of his Son — an act of peace, a restoration of the God / human relationship, by a faithful God.

I believe God intended faith to be a relational concept. He uses marriage to describe His faithfulness with His people and calls us to live in faithfulness to Him. We can have confidence in His character and know in the depths of our souls that He will always be faithful — certain of His love, compassion, and kindness.

It is one thing to believe in someone, and it is quite another to trust them with your very life. In the simplest illustration, I believe that there are several tightrope walkers who can push a wheelbarrow full of bricks across a great chasm — but I am **NOT** going to get in the wheelbarrow! Sadly, many people believe that God can save them, but most people are unwilling to get in the wheelbarrow.

When Gabriel appeared to Mary in Nazareth (see Luke 1) and told her what God was about to do, she could have responded the way Zechariah did, *"I believe You can do this, but I am not sure You will be able to use me and my wife."* Instead, Mary responded in faith, *"May it be done to me as you have said."* One was spoken by a religious leader who viewed faith from a position of transaction, the other came from a teenage girl who viewed faith from a posture of relationship with God. Which position feels best to you?

I hope that we can read statements about faith in scripture from a relational posture. Wouldn't it change the way we understand healing? Wouldn't it change how we understand salvation? The author of Hebrews (11:6) says this, *"And without faith, it is impossible to please God…"*

To engage belief and truth with our wills in our faith journey is a great place to start to repair our relational position with God. And as we do so, our faith grows into certainty, confidence, trust, and security. And we will find ourselves transformed into (not-quite-perfect) faithful children of a faithful God.

~ **Pastor Kurt**

Joy
Week Five

Dec 11 — 17

(Semi-finals and Third-place Match)

Discovering True Joy

Have you ever stopped to consider the shepherds? I mean, why all the fuss? Why are they the first to be told of Jesus' birth? Luke's Gospel captures a unique glimpse at this strange cast of characters receiving amazing news and hurrying to see. Shepherds held a unique place in ancient society. They were, typically, of low social status and importance; they were futureless. Youngest, smallest, childless, they had no inheritance or wealth. They had to scratch out a meager existence watching sheep. Shepherds had no power, position, or legacy. So when the angel comes and announces a son, a Savior has been born, that hopeless future shifts.

As a football chaplain, I've met many who feel hopeless about their future. Many leave the beautiful game feeling hopeless. Wage gaps. Academy players failing to become professional. Young footballers forced into medical retirement. Wealthy, successful footballers who lose everything with gambling addictions or frivolous spending. 99.9% of footballers need second careers. While not social outcasts, footballers can end up feeling hopeless. **When that occurs, it's a real joy killer!**

Today, perhaps you need a messenger delivering *"good news of great joy."* Maybe your agent ringing you with a new

---

Week 5 | Kickoff

Luke 2:10-11

"The angel said to them, 'I bring you great news of great joy...Today...a Savior has been born to you...he is Christ the Lord..."

—

"Joy to the world, the Lord has come; let earth receive her King..."

— from *Joy to the World*, English Christmas carol, Isaac Watts (1719)

contract? The doctor texting that the scans are clear and you'll be back playing soon? Maybe your love just said yes to marriage and this crazy journey of football life? What message might move you to *"hurry"* along and seek?

It's difficult to know where to find joy. It seems like a lifelong chase. We try many things. We experiment with drugs and alcohol, sex, relationships, workaholism, power trips, religion, and more. C. S. Lewis once said,

Joy is not a substitute for sex; sex is very often a substitute for Joy. I sometimes wonder whether all pleasures are not substitutes for Joy. All Joy reminds. It is never a possession, always a desire for something longer ago or further away or still 'about to be'.

Lewis hints at an elusiveness with joy, but usually we mistake pleasure for it. Pleasures are temporary, carnal, leaving us unsatisfied and wanting more. Pleasures feel good, don't get me wrong! But they lessen in satisfaction over time. Desires increase rather than being satiated.

We spend much of life pursuing some way to possess joy. But what if joy isn't something to be obtained as much as something that keeps us searching? If joy is a *"desire for something longer ago or further away or still 'about to be,'"* then it likely is an echo of something deeper, more spiritual — maybe something we cannot fully grasp in this lifetime.

Next week, one team will hoist the World Cup. One nation will be overjoyed. But even the glow and glory of the World Cup is a momentary pleasure. People of football and people of faith **must** look beyond the Cup to the deeper, more eternal reality it points to. And when we do, true Joy will be found.

~ **Rev Brad**

Rejoice, Always. And Then, Rejoice!

If you've never done so, I encourage you to read Paul's letter to the Church at Philippi (also known as the book of Philippians) start to finish. It's only four short chapters. In this letter, Paul uses the word joy (or a derivation of the word such as rejoice) many times.

Week 5 | Halftime

Philippians 4:4

"Rejoice in the Lord, always. I will say it again: rejoice!" (NLT)

—

"There is not one blade of grass, there is no color in this world that is not intended to make us rejoice."

— *John Calvin*

The biblical passages may sound like a self-help, motivational, morning pep-talk . . . and in a sense, they are. However, when you consider Paul wrote this letter while he was in prison, and he is writing to the people of Philippi, who were enduring persecution for their faith in Jesus Christ, it makes you wonder, how can Paul continually write about joy amidst such circumstances?

It's because he didn't focus on his hardships. He focused on God. He rejoiced because he knew that being a Christian does not necessarily mean life will be easy. There will always be testing. There will always be strenuous activity. It does not mean escape. It bears repeating: to know God through Christ is not a promise of an easy life. In many parts of the world, it guarantees persecution to some degree.

So why do so many commit their lives to Christ, and do so joyfully? Because faith in Christ brings true joy. Not the fading happiness that a new car or fancy new house brings, but the joy of having an intimate relationship with the Creator of the earth and the heavens, the joy of knowing that eternity in close fellowship with God awaits, the ability to find joy in all circumstances, and the strength to love your neighbor as yourself (Mark 12:28-34). In all your difficult circumstances, don't despair! Be joyful! Joy is one of the great Christian virtues and the fruit of God's Spirit.

In a few days, one team will know the inexplicable happiness of winning the World Cup, a truly great honor and achievement. This will be accomplished through moments of pain, anguish, disappointment, and all the other emotions that the entire run to the World Cup will inevitably bring. The highs and the lows, and the frustrations of poor execution on the pitch, imprecise refereeing, and maybe even coaching errors. But in the end, with the big win, all will be forgotten. The winning team will bring joy to the supporters, their nation, and all those who invested time, energy, finances, and more to help the team achieve a truly great thing.

But notice, this joy is transient. It is not true joy — it fades. Yes, all will be happy, but happiness is a virtue of the world. The next Cup run will start again in four years. It has to be done all over again without guaranteed results.

Unspeakable joy comes from a close walk with God. A personal relationship with Christ as Lord and Savior never fades. It is permanent for eternity! No need ever to start over again. It is a joy that lasts forever. I hope that you experience that fulfilling and rewarding experience of life in Christ.

~ Rev Jordan

Elation And Joy

What are those moments in your life when you were filled with overwhelming elation and joy? Maybe it is a wedding day, the birth of a child, or winning the lottery. Maybe it was scoring the winning goal for a championship, or watching your country win their first World Cup. Our circumstances can certainly impact our elation and joy, but I hope your joy is not dependent on results!

Week 5 | Final Whistle

Matthew 6:19-21

"Do not lay up for yourselves treasures on earth...but...in heaven...For where your treasure is, there your heart...also."
(ESV)

—

You can read more about the shepherds' elation and joy in Luke 2.

This week, many people around the world are wallowing in their loss because their hope and faith were rooted in a circumstance or result. Where are we looking for joy and elation? Did you or your team compete in the right way?

Our world seems consumed with the pursuit of happiness through results. We pursue instant gratification and find ourselves seeking satisfaction at the expense of true joy. It is as though we are looking for satisfaction of our thirst at a well of dust.

I would suggest that the process is more important to joy than any result. Doing the right things in the right way will lead to satisfaction — whatever the result is. Sure, there is sadness when we don't get the result we want, but we can know joy and satisfaction in the process. A goal scored with the *"Hand of God"* is not nearly as satisfying as dribbling past six different players to score (thanks to VAR that injustice of the former will never happen again!). Same player, same game, same result — but one gives a different sense of elation and joy because of a satisfaction in the process.

How have you tried to cheat a process only to get a cheap result? There are no shortcuts to obtain a desired result! That is certainly one thing soccer teaches us. It takes commitment, dedication, hard work and perseverance. Players need to be hungry, thirsty, for the win, and they will thus joyfully devote themselves 100% to pursue that outcome. Even then, all that does not guarantee the desired result!

But for those pursuing Christ, the outcome is always guaranteed! Advent is a great time to consider our pursuit of joy and satisfaction. Do you know Jesus said those who hunger and thirst for righteousness will be satisfied? He also said that if we seek first His Kingdom and its righteousness, everything else will be taken care of. Seeking happiness and elation at the expense of righteousness is never a good idea and will not bring satisfaction.

There are lots of stories of people finding elation and joy in the Christmas story — from children being born to salvation offered to the least likely of people. But we also see people finding fleeting joy in the materialism of Christmas. "*Do not lay up for yourselves treasures on earth, . . . but lay up for yourselves treasures in heaven . . . For where your treasure is, there your heart will be also*" (Matthew 6:19-21, ESV).

Where is your heart? How are we seeking elation and joy this Christmas? If it is in the right place, we will respond wonderfully in praise and worship of God.

~ **Pastor Kurt**

Peace

Week Six

Dec 18 — 24

(World Cup Final and Christmas Eve)

Peace You Can't Understand

Today is the day! The World Cup Final! Soon all the energy and fervor built into this edition of the World Cup tournament will come to rest. With Christmas Day a week away, perhaps many are looking forward to the relative moment of *"peace"* when the tournament finally ends. I recall a footballer who was so anxious before every match, he would get sick to his stomach and throw up. It didn't matter if it was a regular league match or playoffs — he couldn't experience peace until the opening whistle blew, and the game officially got underway.

Week 6 | Kickoff

Luke 2:14;
Philippians 4:7

"Glory to God in the highest, and on earth peace to those on whom his favor rests."

—

"And the peace of God which transcends all understanding will guard your hearts and minds in Christ Jesus."

The older I become, the more I desire peace. Peace within my home, peace within my city, my country, the world — the list goes on. I remember where I was September 11, 2001. It was a strange day. I wondered if the world would ever see peace again. Of late, the global pandemic, the Ukraine invasion and war by Russia, and so many other moments of conflict and tension have me wondering. I have dear friends in Ciudad Juárez living through and enduring the violence of drug cartels. Many I know in football, especially from Africa and Asia, have had their lives changed and uprooted by war and violence — they have fled continent and country to seek a better life, a more peaceful life.

As a follower of Jesus, I have come to understand that there is a keen difference in what the world promotes as peace and what is (in scripture) known as the peace of God. The world's sense of peace is more about rest and quiet. The transcending peace of God means that even in the midst of conflict and turmoil a person can feel at rest and at peace. A song of many years ago described it this way: *"Sometimes He {God} calms the storm and other times He calms His child."* The peace of God is about an inner mind and soul kind of peace. It cannot be purchased, manufactured, or manipulated. It is a peace which *"passes understanding."* Maybe you've seen it in a fellow footballer or friend. They go through something utterly devastating, utterly shaking, and it's not that they don't express emotion or anger or hurt, but they have a sense of stability and peace despite what they are going through.

What is your experience of peace? Is there an idyllic setting that you pine or hope for? Have you experienced a peace like the peace of God described in scripture? Has your family, your country, your people, been touched by war? Is it difficult for you to experience peace because of racism, sexism, ageism, or other forms of persecution and discrimination?

We are a broken world because we have not restored right relationships with God, with our neighbor, with the created order, and even with our self. Authentic and lasting peace eludes us. Christ came to restore all relationships and shower us with true peace that is truly beyond our understanding.

Until that opening whistle blows...   **~ Rev Brad**

Not A Forced Peace

Imagine it is halftime now. Are you at peace with your team's performance during the first half? What would you tell your team in the locker room?

Week 6 | Halftime

John 14:27

"I am leaving you with a gift — peace of mind and heart. And the peace I give is a gift the world cannot give. So don't be troubled or afraid."
(NLT)

—

"If God be our God, He will give us peace in trouble. When there is a storm without, He will make peace within. The world can create trouble in peace, but God can create peace in trouble."

— Thomas Watson

In today's world, the word peace generally means an absence of conflict or war. It's usually a sign you make with your first and second finger in the shape of a "V" when taking a selfie or other picture to post on social media. It's something younger generations say when leaving a gathering. It's a hope or a dream that wars would cease, arguments would never happen, and everybody would just get along.

For the past 3,400 years, there have only been 268 total years where there were no wars. **That's 8%.**

The famous *"Pax Romana"* or Roman Peace of the Roman empire, from the outside looks like a long period of relative peace throughout the ancient world. However, *"Pax Imperia"* may be a better description of those times, an imperial or forced peace brought on by the sheer power of the Roman government. It lasted for two hundred years, and the narrative of Jesus Christ occurred during the early part of that period (27 BC – 180 AD).

This Advent we celebrate a coming offer of true peace to all who believe (in Christ) and the joyful expectation of peace forever with God in heaven. This is why Jesus told his best friends, *"I am leaving you with a gift — peace of mind and heart. And the peace I give is a gift the world cannot give. So don't be troubled or afraid"* (John 14:27, NLT). Relationship with Jesus means peace for his followers and friends.

Peace also comes from knowing there is a God in heaven who has known you and loved you since the beginning of time, and when we walked away from him in sin, he offered a way back to peace with him through the blood of Jesus Christ. He offers us eternal fellowship with him. Until then, God has given us the gift of prayer to lay all our worries, fears, burdens, and anxieties before Him to restore our peace.

This peace that surpasses all [human] understanding (Philippians 4:7), is a peace that nothing in this world can give us. Peace not forced upon us, though he has the power and authority to do so, but peace offered to us as a choice.

"Don't worry about anything; instead, pray about everything. Tell God what you need, and thank him for all he has done. Then you will experience God's peace, which exceeds anything we can understand. His peace will guard your hearts and minds as you live in Christ Jesus...Keep putting into practice all you learned and received from me — everything you heard from me and saw me doing. Then the God of peace will be with you" (Philippians 4:6-9, NLT).

Let this halftime, this pause in the game, be a time to reflect about God's beautiful offer of unforced peace.

~ Rev Jordan

Fearless Or Courageous?

We know that fear is natural and a gift that keeps us from dangerous behavior. If you have no fear of heights, you may walk off a cliff. If you have no fear of fire, you may burn to death. If you have no fear of pain, you may cut your hand off. If you have no fear of people, then you may be taken advantage of.

Fear is valuable, but there is clearly a difference between **invigorating** fear and **debilitating** fear.

I love watching sports — virtually every sport requires courage for success. We admire the quarterback who stands and delivers in the face of severe danger. We admire the tennis player who risks a passing shot down the line. We are impressed by the footballer who risks criticism for blasting a shot off a cross without using a touch to settle the ball. We say they are brave.

Bravery is not the absence of fear, but it is doing something despite the fear. If there is no fear, then it isn't bravery, it is just plain arrogance.

Throughout the Christmas story we see fear — particularly related to the appearance of angels. People believed the appearance of an angel meant they were about to meet their Maker. It would be a dreadful thing to see one

Week 6 | Final Whistle

Philippians 4:9

"Whatever you have learned or received or heard from me, or seen in me—put it into practice. And the God of peace will be with you."

—

Read Paul's letter to the Philippians; particularly chapter 4, verses 4-7. What are some steps to experiencing a peace that surpasses your circumstances?

who shines like the sun and speaks with the voice of God. This is why, angels appear with a common voice: *"Fear not, be courageous."*

Many years earlier, we hear similar words spoken to Joshua, *"Be bold and courageous; do not be terrified."* The courageous behavior was to do all that God had commanded him. The same is true for each person in the Christmas story. To only do what God has commanded is to be of good courage and bold in our faith, despite what appears to be a losing proposition.

For those who are courageous despite their fears, to those are given peace. To receive peace, we need to trust in God – people of faith are able to live in abundance in the face of fear. We know that we are in the hands of God, and because of Jesus, this is a good thing. Therefore, no matter what the situation, we are of good courage and have peace.

I wonder what the players on the pitch have felt throughout the World Cup? Fear or courage? If they had been faithful in their preparations, their fear will have been **invigorating**. But if they had been slacking off, they likely suffer a **debilitating** fear, a condition that exposed all of their weaknesses and lack of preparedness. They will have been unable to be courageous. And that is a bad psychological place to be in anytime, but especially in the pressure cooker of the World Cup competition.

What fears are you facing with courage today? How are you experiencing peace in the face of adversity? How have preparations been going to help you face this current challenge with a joyful confidence?   **~ Pastor Kurt**

Love

Week Seven

Dec 25 – 31

(Christmas Day and New Year's Eve)

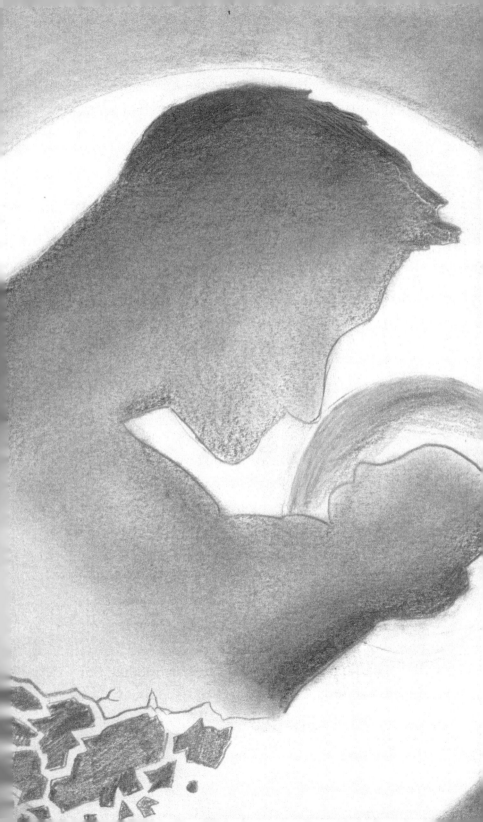

Love, G.O.A.T.

Merry Christmas! Today is monumental because we celebrate the birth and first *"adventus"* (arrival) of Jesus so many years ago. His birth is a sign of God's love and care for the world. His life, death, and resurrection are all part of God's plan to reconcile His relationship with people that was broken and severed back in the idyllic Garden of Eden. But why is love the greatest of all time (G.O.A.T.)?

Week 7 | Kickoff

John 3:16;

I Corinthians 13:13

"For God so loved the world that he gave his one and only Son, that whoever believes in him shall not perish but have eternal life."

—

*"And now these three remain: faith, hope and **love**. But the greatest of these is **love**."*

We've already mentioned faith finishing in the top three and hope coming in second, but why does Paul say that love is the greatest of the three Christian theological virtues?

Simply put, it's because of the eternality of love. We see God's love and care in the beginning — at creation, even at the fall of humankind — God's love makes the first sacrifice, He clothes His precious fallen people Adam and Eve as representative of all of humanity. And then His love clothes His redeemed people in the perfect righteousness of Jesus Christ. So love wins out not because of its role in the beginning, but its place in the end.

Remember, faith becomes sight. Hope is fulfilled. But love, **love never ends**. The last pages of scripture declare God's dwelling place finally and for all time to be in loving relationship with His beloved children. In the end, love remains for all eternity. Love has no end, it goes on and on. I find it difficult at times to wrap my mind around this idea.

Maybe it's easier to consider one of the strongest and simplest images of love — the love of a mother for her child. Consider Mary's love of Jesus — if we had time and space to list all that she went through and endured in pregnancy, in life, after Jesus' death, resurrection, and ascension — it's amazing to me all that she endured as an example of love.

The greatest example of love, though, is exemplified by Jesus. He told his best friends that the greatest love happens when one lays *"down one's life for one's friends"* (John 15:13). Jesus did this. Jesus tells his followers, his friends, to do this and keep doing it.

Has anyone ever laid down their life for you? Maybe they didn't step in front of a bullet or push you out of the way of an oncoming train, but maybe they gave up something or made a sacrifice for you. I've seen parents work multiple jobs for a child to be able to play. I've seen teammates step aside to let someone else score the goal and take the glory. I've watched humble coaches praise players and deflect attention away from themselves. I've watched partners and spouses leave jobs, families, and familiarity for the unknown aspects of football. Much of this comes from a place of human love; God's love is infinitely greater!

Today, as you ponder love that you've experienced — in football, in family, in faith — consider how that warrants a response. Read and reflect on I John 4:7 – 5:12. Consider God's great love for us in making the ultimate sacrifice, and how His love is the greatest of all time (G.O.A.T.). **~ Rev Brad**

Looking For Love...In All The Right Places?

We are all looking to love and be loved. Over 60% of songs in the history of songwriting were written about love.

Some of my personal favorites are:

"Can't Buy Me Love" by the Beatles, which expresses a willingness to set aside everything else for love.

"At Last" by Etta James, rejoices in the relief brought by the love that has finally come to fruition.

"Can't Stop the Feeling" by Justin Timberlake, delights in the elation of being around a person we have a deep connection with.

While *"Ain't No Mountain High Enough"* by Marvin Gaye and Tammi Terrell, celebrates the strong bond of love and commitment.

Each song describes the feeling we receive from another person, and we call it love.

However, God demonstrates that love is not about the rush of endorphins we may feel when we are around a person we are attracted to. *"God's love,"* says H.W. Hoehner, *"is seeking the highest good in the one loved."* The Christian scriptures say this: *"For this is how God loved the world: He gave his one and only Son, so that everyone who believes in him will not perish but have eternal life"* (John 3:16, NLT).

Some Christians attempt to present a gospel witness in stadiums and arenas by holding up signs displaying the gospel message of John 3:16. You may have even seen it on an athlete's undershirt, exposed when the jersey was lifted in triumph after a goal was scored. Most commonly, the message will be very short — **JN 3:16** — with a hope that people will get a bible and read the verse.

This is to divert people from acting on their natural tendency of desperately searching to find the authentic love we seek through possessions or settling for the closest thing we can find to love. We enter casual relationships, we experience cheap thrills, thinking that these efforts will fill the void. We create false messiahs (saviors) out of money, cars, power, trophies, honors, and even other people, such as celebrities or gurus, claiming to know how to find love. This is not the case with true love, God's love. We only know what true love is from God.

"Dear friends, let us continue to love one another, for love comes from God. Anyone who loves is a child of God and knows God. But anyone who does not love does not know God, for God is love" (1 John 4:7-8, NLT).

Advent and Christmas are celebrations of Christ's first coming as a baby and the expectation of His return one day. It is all about God's unfathomable love — that love whereby He took upon himself the form of a human and died as our sacrifice. It is worth repeating: God demonstrated love by giving Jesus, not only as our exemplar, but as a sacrifice for our sins. Accepting and receiving God's love through Jesus is the only love that can truly satisfy. **~ Rev Jordan**

For The Love...

You have probably heard many speak or write about *"Finding your 'WHY?'"* You may have your "WHY?", and you may even have it rooted in love — which is the key to any "WHY?"!

Week 7 | Final Whistle

I John 4:10

"This is love: not that we loved God, but that he loved us and sent his Son as an atoning sacrifice..."

—

Read I John

Everything we do is rooted in love. I eat because I love food! I drink coffee because I love the flavor — and the caffeine. I get up in the morning because I love, and I am loved. I serve as a pastor of a church because I love people. I serve God because I am loved by Him. I do chores because . . . well, I do chores!

I would suggest that even the most mundane of tasks, practices, activities, and even chores can be, and should be, rooted in love. This becomes our "WHY?"

If you are struggling to find purpose or meaning in your life, come back to the question of, *"What and whom do I love enough to keep going?"* Or, *"Who loves me enough to keep me going?"*

The younger you are, the more the second question motivates us. The more mature you become, the question becomes about how we are loving others. Ultimately, it all comes down to how much God loves us, and how His love motivates and inspires us to love others.

Jesus' "WHY?" was, and is, love. The Father's "WHY?" was, and is, love. And the Holy Spirit's "WHY?" is love as well. He is love and out of love gives us spiritual life so that we can relate to God. And the proof that we belong to God is seen in our love towards one another, for God is love — Father, Son, and Holy Spirit.

When we come to the end of a tournament, a season, or a life-stage, we are all faced with the need to find our "WHY?" Sadly, many flounder in the doldrums while they are searching. For some, it is for the love of the game that they press on. For others, it is for the love of the crowd. For still others, it is the love of endorphins that they get from the rush. For all these people, the target of their love is themselves. But true love is directed toward God and toward our neighbor. So for a few, the answer to their "WHY?" is for the love of God, and they sense the call from Him to press on. Typically, for this same group of people, their sense of "WHY?" is driven by a love and compassion for others above self — purely deflected from a sense of the Father's love for us.

Read the Apostle John's first letter to the Church. It is super short, but there is a common theme throughout — **LOVE**. It is written by an old man who, along with his brother, were called *"the sons of thunder"* when they were much younger. When he wrote his gospel about Jesus, John referred to himself several times in the story as *"the disciple whom Jesus loved"* (John 19:26, 20:2, 21:7, 21:20, ESV). I think John found his "WHY?" and he calls the Church to do the same in his letter to the Church (see I John).

What is your "WHY?" for 2023?

~ **Pastor Kurt**

Worship

Week Eight

Jan 1 – 7

(New Year's Day and Epiphany)

We've Come To Worship

I love the etymology (fancy word for origin) of the word *"worship."* It's from the old English *"worth ship"* meaning to ascribe worthiness, or to acknowledge one's value.

The Magi arrive after Jesus' birth, and their visit really stirs things up. They announce they've come to worship the newborn king. Maybe they're surprised that no one else is really in the celebrating and party mood? What ensues are secret meetings, deception, fear-mongering, threat, scandal, and espionage. The beautiful story of Jesus' birth turns into a full-scale, international, suspense thriller with storylines including a dream-led detour for the Magi, a midnight flight into foreign lands by Jesus' family, and the tragic murder of Jesus' boyhood buddies. But amidst the drama, let's not lose sight of the Magi's attitude and posture of worship.

Week 8 | Kickoff

Matthew 2:2, 11

"Where is the one who has been born king of the Jews? We saw his star in the East and have come to worship him."

—

"On coming to the house, they saw the child with his mother Mary, and they bowed down and worshipped him."

Notice, the Magi were seeking. *"We saw his star in the East..."* We don't know their time of arrival, but the text suggests a fair amount of time passing. They were probably researching, and studying the night skies for many years. Something about this star and the Hebrew prophecies impacted them enough to set out on the journey.

The journey: we don't know how far exactly, but we know they had come some distance. This likely came at great personal expense. They probably had an entourage. Travel was tough, not like today — it took endurance and patience.

Additionally, the Magi brought expressions of worship. They bowed down — a personal expression. They brought gifts — a longer-lasting expression. Each gift holding its own unique meaning and significance.

Relay this into our recent experience of the World Cup. How much researching, studying, waiting, and anticipation for this event? How many making the long journey to Qatar? Consider ascriptions of worth — tickets purchased, accommodations booked, songs sung, sacrifices (time off work, etc.) made, cheers and celebrations. Acts of worship typically involve all of our being — our bodies, our postures, our finances, our voices, our hearts, minds, and souls.

What things, today, do we ascribe worth to? What things do we worship? Jesus once said, *"Where your treasure is, there your heart will be also"* (Matthew 6:21). Where are our hearts? A football club or national team? In a career or climbing the ladder? In a relationship — a spouse, a partner, a child, or other loved one? Where is Jesus, in relation to our worship? Do we give ourselves to Him — heart, mind, body, and soul? Or do we reserve a scant amount of time, thought, treasure, and talent for the King of Kings and the Lord of Lords?

This New Year, let us approach the worship of Jesus as the Magi of long ago did. Yes, there is a cost; there are sacrifices to be made; there are expressions and gifts we must willingly offer up. But Jesus is worth it. Let us ascribe all worth and worthiness due His name!

~ **Rev Brad**

New Beginnings

The World Cup is now well in our rear view. We've been through our Christmas and Advent celebrations and our New Year's Eve celebrations. We've made our New Year's resolutions. Maybe you are starting off the year with everything you could dream of. Maybe you are starting off the year with a World Cup Victory, or at least a victory in your eyes by reaching beyond the group stage, or reaching the quarterfinals, semi-finals, or even the final, itself.

This time of year is all about new beginnings. This time in the church calendar is called Epiphany as we celebrate the Magi and the gifts they brought to the baby Jesus, and what these meant.

Contrary to popular belief, the Magi were not present the night Jesus was born. Scholars debate exactly when the Magi arrived, but best we can tell it was most likely between forty days and two years after Jesus' birth.

While we may not know the exact time the Magi visited Jesus, we do know they brought three very important gifts: gold, frankincense, and myrrh.

The gift of gold acknowledged Jesus as royalty, the King of Kings, and Lord of Lords. So gold was an appropriate gift for the new King.

The gift of frankincense represented the sacrificial nature of Christ's mission from God. Frankincense was often used to create a pleasing aroma before the Lord during Old Testament sacrifices. Frankincense acknowledged the once and for all sacrifice of Christ Jesus. It is fitting now that Christ Jesus is *"our merciful and faithful High Priest before God"* (Hebrews 2:17, NLT).

The gift of myrrh also points to the death of Christ as a sacrifice. Myrrh was the main ingredient in the anointing oil used to prepare the altar for a sacrifice (Exodus 30:26-29). This gift foreshadowed Christ's sacrificial death.

But what does that have to do with you and me?

The Magi, who were *"wise men,"* thought they knew everything, thought they had it all figured out, yet were still searching. The Magi, when they knew that God was calling them (the star in the East), were obedient to that calling and came to Christ Jesus. Their natural course of action was to lay it all before the Lord Jesus.

God is calling you. God is calling you to acknowledge Christ as King and offer your gifts of time, talent, and treasure in worship to him. In whatever you do, glorify God. If you are a player, play as if playing for the Lord, train as if training for the Lord. If you are a coach, coach as if coaching for the Lord, lead as if leading for the Lord. If you are an administrator, organize and manage as if managing for the Lord. Offer your time in service to His Kingdom. Offer your talents in service to His Kingdom. Offer the treasures of your heart and all that you are in service to His Kingdom.

~ Rev Jordan

The Worship Of Nations

The last two months have shown us that the nations worship football, soccer, or fútbol. When I was in Australia studying the Church, one pastor told me, *"The national religion of Australia is sport — not a specific one, just sport."* On a visit to Europe, a pastor in Europe said that the favorite sport of Europe is not football, but betting or gambling. Is anyone surprised that the World Cup competed with Advent for the love and attention of the world — and won? Football is by far the largest spectator sport in the world. And for comparison, American football ranks 9th!

When you consider the events surrounding the Christmas story, are you surprised how few people recognized that the King of the Jews had been born? The very heavens declared His birth for all to see! Do you realize that God declared the birth of His Son in such a way that the pagan nations of the world would see and know the King had been born. But only a few were watching, paying attention, and waiting for a revelation.

The nations came bearing gifts of worship. Their worship was not defined by their gifts, but their gifts were defined by their worship. What gifts are you bringing the King of Kings? Are you bringing them from a place of worship? Or are you withholding your worship because of what you have or don't have to offer?

Remember the story of the poor widow who put only a couple of cents into the Temple treasury while others gave much more? Jesus pointed her out and told his disciples that she gave more than anyone else, because she gave out of her poverty; others gave out of their riches.

What if I were to tell you that everything you do is worship? Would it not then become a question of 'who' or 'what' you are worshipping instead of simply 'whether'? When we reread the story of the Magi, is it any wonder why the Father would choose to reveal His Son's birth to them?

Authentic worship is always in response to the revelation of God. Unfortunately, too many people around the world are not watching or listening for Him. It is our job to call people's attention to Him and to offer every aspect of our lives to Him in worship. It's in this way we can stop worshiping football and begin to **worship Him with football**. As the Teacher once said and the Apostle Paul built upon, *"Whatever your hand [or foot] finds to do, do it with all your might as though you are doing it for the Lord."* (paraphrase of Ecclesiastes 9:10 and Colossians 3:23, ESV)

Your worship does not need to be money, incense, or spices. The best that you can offer the King of Kings and High Priest of Priests is yourself. As you lay yourself on the altar in worship, He is glorified and honored. As you worship Him, He will reveal more to you about Himself.

Come and worship. Worship Christ the Newborn King!

~ Pastor Kurt

Acknowledgements

From Rev Brad

Jesus Christ — Lord and Savior, You are the Light of the world. Thanks for inviting each of us to follow and be reflective of Your light. Your life is light to me. Thank You for coming and promising to come again.

Adriana — thank you for allowing me to pursue this life calling to reflect light to the world of football. I know it hasn't been easy. I love you.

Brianna, Caley, Danielle, and Allison — my beautiful daughters. You bring me joy and laughter, thank you for believing in me and loving me.

Mom and Dad — thanks for your unwavering support and love over the years.

Those in Football (Soccer) — the Beautiful Game has taken me far and wide and I am privileged to have befriended so many from around the globe. I pray that you will know that the Light is coming!

Specific to this book

Gregory Aydt — thanks for reviewing our spelling, grammar, and theology, you are the Comma King! Your heart to Defend Memphis and Memphis 901 FC has no equal…now to work on your disc golf game.

Jim Barnard — thanks for all your help and giving selflessly of your time and energy in figuring out Amazon, KDP, etc. Keep on tilling! I promise more than a Meserve lunch as thanks. God bless tillercoaching.org.

Stella Bertsch — you are a gifted young woman and artist. Thank you for sharing your gifts with us.

Fraser Keay — best mate! Thanks for encouraging me when I thought this project was dead in the water. May God bless your publishing work through illuminepress.org and may Scotland make the next World Cup!

Acknowledgements (cont.)

Caley Kenney — you are a beautiful young woman and a talented and creative artist. You are a strong leader and I am proud to be your dad.

Jubal McDaniel — thank you for your work toward the design and layout of the book. Tacoma Defiance is blessed to have you as chaplain.

Jordan Medas — thank you for your pastor's heart toward the people of your church and of soccer that God has divinely put you into their lives.

Mike Sares — thank you for allowing me to sit in the "chair of consolation" and learn from you about creating Advent and Christmas guides. God bless your work with UrbanSkye.org and all you do.

Kiera Thielke — you are a gifted artist and wonderful young woman. Thank you for sharing your gifts with us!

Kurt Trempert — thank you for your wit and wisdom (debatable which you have more of) that comes out in your writings. You are honest and open. Thank you for your heart for Colorado Springs Switchbacks FC.

Jan van Vliet — thank you for your time and energy to edit the book in the midst of your own deadlines and writing projects. Blessed to know you. We will see how Netherlands do this World Cup!

From Rev Jordan

To my lovely wife, Lisa, and our four wonderful children, Jonah, Abby, Jessi, and Molly — thank you for your unconditional love and support of me at all times.

Rev. Adam Colson, Bill and Bobbie Fetzer, and The Lake of the Woods Church — thank you for your continued support of my work in ministry to athletes and coaches, particularly in the soccer community.

Social and Connecting

soccerchaplainsunited.org

app: SoccerChapUtd

iOS

Android

Social and Connecting

PO Box 102081, Denver, CO 80250

info@soccerchaplainsunited.org

@SoccerChaplains

Soccer Chaplains United

Podcast: From the Touchline

About

Soccer Chaplains United is united by a common code and shared vision to provide spiritual care, wise counsel, and meaningful service for soccer.

Our primary emphasis is on chaplaincy development. Our chaplains consider and care for the whole person — whether an athlete, coach, staff member, alumni, fan, or family member. We train our chaplains to pastorally and spiritually care for all those belonging to the greater soccer community — and at all levels of the game.

Soccer Chaplains United also facilitates meaningful service opportunities between the faith and soccer community. Through our Community Project initiatives we resource different groups with new and used soccer gear to effect change locally and globally. Learn more on our website.

Soccer Chaplains United is non-profit, 501(c)3. Our chaplains serve as volunteers and we depend upon the financial support of our partners to carry out our work of developing chaplaincy across all levels of soccer. Please consider making a contribution today to help us continue growing our chaplains and our work in the US and beyond.

Made in the USA
Columbia, SC
16 November 2022

71050609R00046